Whatever We Are

Whatever We Are

Eva Kolacz

First Edition

The John B. Lee Signature Series

Hidden Brook Press
www.HiddenBrookPress.com
writers@HiddenBrookPress.com

Copyright © 2019 Hidden Brook Press
Copyright © 2019 Eva Kolacz

All rights for poems revert to the author. All rights for book, layout and design remain with Hidden Brook Press. No part of this book may be reproduced except by a reviewer who may quote brief passages in a review. The use of any part of this publication reproduced, transmitted in any form or by any means, electronic, mechanical, photocopied, recorded or otherwise stored in a retrieval system without prior written consent of the publisher is an infringement of the copyright law.

Whatever We Are
by Eva Kolacz

Editor – John B. Lee
Cover Art: Eva Kolacz, painting, "Phase of Light 1" (2008)
Cover Design – Richard M. Grove
Layout and Design – Richard M. Grove

Typeset in Garamond
Printed and bound in Canada
Distributed in USA by Ingram, in Canada by Hidden Brook Distribution

Library and Archives Canada Cataloguing in Publication

Title: Whatever we are / Eva Kolacz.
Names: Kolacz, Eva, author.
Description: First edition. | Poems.
Identifiers: Canadiana 20190076593 | ISBN 9781927725672 (softcover)
Classification: LCC PS8621.O467 W53 2019 | DDC C811/.6—dc23

" . . .and this our life, when was it truly ours?
and when are we truly whatever we are?"

Octavio Paz *Sun Stone*

To my mother,
Patty and Laurence

Acknowledgements:

Some of these poems have appeared in the League of Canadian Poets' *Feminist Newsletter*, *Verse Afire*, *The Artis,* and the anthologies *Things That Matter* and *Tamaracks: Canadian Poetry for the 21st Century*.

I would like to thank John B. Lee, the editor of my manuscript for his vision in shaping it. I want to thank Richard Grove (Tai) for designing and publishing this book.

A special gratitude goes to my mother, who was the force behind my art and writing throughout my life and to my daughter, Patty for her support and skilful advice. I would especially like to thank my husband, Laurence—without you this book would not be the same.

Table of Contents

Acknowledgements – *p. xi*
Introduction by John B. Lee – *p. vix*

– Inquiry into Pastoral Life – *p. 2*
– Places Beyond Words – *p. 4*
– In the Maze of Lines – *p. 5*
– Blue Heron – *p. 6*
    1. Dream
    2. Ambience
    3. Levitation
– Continuity – *p. 9*
– Pink Room – *p. 10*
– Goodbye – *p. 11*
– Something About Darkness – *p. 12*
– Exodus – *p. 13*
– Refuge – *p. 14*
– Solving Algebra Equations – *p. 15*
– Change Needs to Know Me – *p. 16*
– Exhibiting bold facts – *p. 17*
– The Voice of a Bird in Very Early Morning – *p. 18*
– Being (with) Fiction, Touching Poetry – *p. 19*
– Flight – *p. 20*
– Rain in the Room with Mountain – *p. 21*
– Image-Makers – *p. 22*
– Into the New World – *p. 23*
– Crossing the Border into Manitoba – *p. 24*
– Pause in Time – *p. 26*
– If These Lines Could Sing – *p. 27*
– I lack the Inspired Silence – *p. 28*
– Apocalypse – *p. 29*
– I Was Rescued by Raw Animal Instinct – *p. 30*
– Walk through Conversation – *p. 31*
– Climb and Dream – *p. 32*
– Disconnecting the Link – *p. 33*
– Mission – *p. 34*

– Flying the Dream – *p. 35*
– Lizard's Song – *p. 36*
– In the End of Summer – *p. 37*
– Gypsy Love – *p. 38*
– Love Affair (projected as tragic) – *p. 39*
– Back to Freud's Dream – *p. 40*
– Oceans of Drifting Sand – *p. 41*
– A Dance on the Roof – *p. 42*
– Wild Horses – *p. 43*
– Bogoria – *p. 44*
– Walking Among the Birds – *p. 45*
– Romancing the Painting – *p. 46*
– Real Life Drawing – *p. 47*
– Mindfulness of Lake Ontario – *p. 48*
– Bee Caught in Amber – *p. 49*
– Morning Talk in Oakville – *p. 50*
– Drowned in a Hollow Moon – *p. 51*
– The Blueprint of a Lake – *p. 52*
– The Tree Dries to Dust – *p. 53*
– The Buried Side of Childhood
    1. The Side – *p. 54*
    2. The Final Inquest – *p. 54*
    3. The King, the Court – *p. 55*
    4. The End or Consolation – *p. 55*
– The Narrow Pathway of Childhood – *p. 56*
– Walking the Night – *p. 58*
– Each of Us – *p. 59*
– We Are All Immigrants on This Planet – *p. 60*
– All These Moments of Difficult Truth – *p. 61*
– Shreds of Thoughts – *p. 62*
– Moving with the Current – *p. 63*

Bio Note – *p. 65*

The past sometimes appears as a dreamer...
"Exhibiting Bold Facts"

On the way travelling between Bardstown Kentucky and the Trappist monastery Abby of Gethsemani there sits a rough-looking roadhouse. Three fellow Canadian poets and I were intrigued by the look of it in passing, though one of our number was fearful of the dangers we might encounter therein. He said of himself that he was only clad in sandals and that he wished he were wearing his steel-toed boots lest he need defend us from the fracas that would surely occur if we dared to enter the darkness. Despite his trepidation, we stopped and swaggered in wearing our Canadian flag T-shirts. We bellied up to the bar where a newspaper lay open on which the words "metaphysics" and "existentialism" were scribbled in pencil by some local hand. Someone had scribed those words and given them each a simple definition.

"Existentialism and Metaphysics indeed!" dear reader you might well ask, "What does this have to do with the poetry of Eva Kolacz?" *Everything and nothing.* Her book *Whatever We Are* begins with an epigram from American poet Muriel Rukeyser's translation of Nobel Laureate Octavio Paz's magnum opus the poem "Sun Stone". She quotes the lines "...and this our life, when was it truly ours?/and when are we truly whatever we are?"

The poems of Eva Kolacz are those of a poet whose memories are a blend of fondness and sadness, whose experience in exile are a blend of alienation and belonging, whose dreams are those of delight and pain, whose imaginings are those of angst and joy, a poet who deals with the big questions with clarifying complexity and all-embracing simplicity. Like the Aztec calendar of Paz's poem "Sun Stone" she engages the reader with images of sun and moon—the sun burns while the moon dreams. We are drawn into a world where brutality is calmed by understanding and where life is embraced in all its aspects. Her poems range from erotic engagements of female desire to the dark side of sexuality as manifest in violence and danger. The big questions we ask, the ones we ask concerning the possible absurdity of human existence and the spiritual realm of divine contemplation are here in glorious relief. Existentialism and metaphysics in poetry, like the big man in the rough looking bar in Kentucky only a few short miles from the Trappist monastery and in the other direction the grow operation house where a local criminal might drive you off his land waving a gun and threatening you for daring to stop and ask for directions. In this world *what are we?*

We might console ourselves by contemplating the words of Eva's final poem in the collection wherein she writes:

> Moving with the Current
>
> Now we who turn our backs on the past,
> feel the years still burning inside of us
>
> though we move with the current of time
> which sometimes contradicts our conception of reason.
>
> Your tongue is destined to be harp-like
> performing poems in the place
> where minds and sounds converge
> to find what is meant to be found.

John B. Lee Poet
Laureate of the city of Brantford in perpetuity
Poet Laureate of Norfolk County for life
Author of over 70 books

Whatever We Are

Inquiry into Pastoral Life
Nobody can bring you peace but yourself.
         Ralph Waldo Emerson

1

Let us have dreams
ripen like fruit a future may not re-call.
Meet me ex-urbanite who left smog & traffic of Toronto
for (no, not exactly)—pastoral life farm animals
are hardly seen

only their shadows dance, jump & shine with ease.
Change becomes us—someone said.
The beginning leaves time behind.
This is what poet & mystic can define
effortlessly.
Behind the tree on the rooftop
crows sampling air under their wings
& swearing in harsh tones
at my unfamiliar face.

2

Mad mad heat put August on the grill,
fields of corn exploding with fire,
dry exhausted sky
days shrink and disappear.
Last night I cut photographs.
Departing has the taste of sadness
the thread broken   connection lost   a filament of ash.

A few of memories will try to reappear again
in our sleep by using camouflage
& wake you up.
Some will turn their faces away from you
and on some you will turn your back on.

Places Beyond Words

Here at home the winds
don't have wings
but they are rushing down the hill
in the manner of a flashing hawk

to touch your arm and pick up grief.
Move to the rhythm of
the stream that leads us along the trees.

That's a real possibility to taste the sun.
Things move and speak,
their existence is of a rising song,
a trumpet bell
dangled in an inner ear of our memory.

Life can be a weathered motionless boat
lying on the back of the sand,
to be turned upside down
in a desire to know what lies beyond

wide open passage of water with drifts
evoking God's wish for us to go
against the highest tide
& saving nothing for later.

Having come so far, be ageless.
Behind you a curved horizon,
grid of light furrows like spoken words.

In the Maze of Lines

They say we have a map of lines
or at least a fraction of it
on the palm of our hands.

In the web of tiny lines we act like birds
destined at birth to follow the path of our ancestors

not knowing yet we are just instruments
needed to compose the songs of life.

With no time on our side and trying for clarity
of this complexity
we walk leaving scattered footprints
over the roads beyond the patterns of failure.

Who are we
when we are born with a silver spoon?
Who are when we are left to survive,
when we are dreaming like flying fish of conquering the sky,
but we end up in a net of our own vulnerability?

Blue Heron
for Natasha

1. Dream

I can hear steps in my dreams
eaten away by dim streets
with clouds shaping the sky
nothing can touch them
not even the saints in heaven.

Existence is constantly proving
that we hold onto a vision
of a better world that is still alive
even if it is taken from
the scattering of history,
letting rivers flow freely
into the face of the sun.

Sometimes we just need
the human helping hand,
at other times God's will,
knowing that everything
could deteriorate again
when touched by a blade of fire.

2. Ambience

Fallen oak leaves
move with the wind
into a place behind the pond,
reclining in tall grasses.
The moment freezes
the flight of a blue heron,
then raises him from the shore
to the temple of the sky.
Words becoming fruit
of thought waiting the phrases
to build a line binding us to nature.

Everything can speak now
awakening us.
Somebody is walking and singing,
then disappears,
but his song remains
caressing our ears.

3. Levitation

Rising out of gravel the fog wanders.
In my dream last night, I was enveloped
in the darkness of nameless streets.
Now I'm an inhabitant of the earth in Oakville
close to the absolute,
when everything around me is simply lifted
as it turns and turns
in slow motion,
until it is out of sight.

Continuity

every moment
has its own sense
of continuity
charged by philosophical questions
concerning
purpose of existence

every moment
driven
by primal instincts   (read: animal)
                  preying on the self
& sometimes
will lure you into a spider's web
sometimes
will lift you like a bird on the wing

when we pause to refresh our minds
the moment continues
like a stream moving
in the channels of the body,
never looking for an exit

Pink Room

Memory says: Want to do right?
Don't Count on me.
                    Adrienne Rich

Room within the room
—little girl's dream.
Ah, subtle allure of pink,
imagination soars
in sweat simple moments,
a twinkle in time.

Now, after passing years she is observing
the formation of her thoughts
twinkle twinkle little star tracking itself
on the sky to find the truth,
what happened
in this place years ago.

Once he gave me a doll,
I didn't understand his touch
which locked me in its darkness
for a long time,
in the thin shape of my existence.
I started to be invisible
the air around me
was not easy to swallow.

They say healing comes
in different ways.
That moment carried me away
toward peaceful presence
of whiteness behind the window
with a lace of snowflakes
on my fingertips
                    wondering.

Goodbye

She stretched her arms toward him
and stopped in the middle of goodbye.

She did not break the silence,
knowing that the air could become impatient.

She remembers the scars that occupied her body
with no visible signs,
and when she became another woman standing alone
maturing in acute awareness of pain.

His mask-like face
was quickly carried away into the street
through cold blue glass of air.

Something About Darkness

She is carefully picking up a cup of latté,
she doesn't want to ruin her dress
flowering in the late spring light.

She is thinking about the past
and watching people rushing like a stream
from behind the Starbucks's window.
She can almost touch them through the glass.

At first, she did not clearly see his actions
no textbook can teach you this,
you can follow all the right rules and
yet get bogged down in the most appealing nonsense.

"There is something about darkness
soon I almost know the place
scattered
crippled
rocking the cradle of my womanhood."

A scar is or could be a paradox—someone said
failure and resilience
at the same time.

Almost no sound came from her lips
when he smashed the wine bottle
and slipped on the wet paving stone.
She was a bird poised for flight.

Exodus

I will feel again the shape of memories
              the volume of line
the mass   I remember
my run from a village with naked air on my arms
                    toward the land of promise
                    and how it turns back on me.

When it comes to this
you will not search
for words
nor dig down to find them buried
up to   the   waist in a ditch
                          of pain.

Hear me
but don't talk
until I howl in anger, spit all of it out
and undo the spell of army men.
                And then teach me
on the way to the rescue team
            how to stich up   the hungry mouth
                  of the falling sky.

Refuge

"Unable to imagine a future
imagine a future better
than now" . . .
   Sharon Thesen, Praxis

The clouds were blind & confused
in their new shape
   of mist with no end or beginning
sinking into our skin drifting
the overcrowded boat moved like a wounded bird.

I'm here
and not here at all
was it my choice not to exist?
&
hanging on a grim-lipped day
trying hard
not to look
at the blood-flushed sunset
flowing into & out of memories swallowed by
smoke of the burning city we left
when dust from the rubble is eating the air
you don't hear your own cry
judge us not
I can't withdraw hope from my life.

At night spikes of hard waves come
        to lift the boat
         & spin it around
          like a slow-motion carousel
I can't find my words anymore
        they're speeding up toward
the surface of the sea covered with bubbled air
of my breath
all I can hear now is the whisper of water
taking me softly in.

Solving Algebra Equations

*Carry on, then, if only for a moment
that it takes a tiny galaxy to blink!*
                    Wislawa Szymborska

I prefer not to comfort the moonless night
gazing at me
with my own mortality, consciously
rather to ignore her pretentious smile
which tries to win me over
by changing my way of thinking.
And remind myself
that this night & I share nothing except morning
morning morning
let me sing foolishly
to see how it gives voice to a new day.

This night & I share nothing except the need
to pursue goals of the ego
forgetting that everything
is endless repetition
the already known.
And life, please, don't make us hungry
for this self-involved importance
unless solving algebraic equations is your thing.

Change Needs to Know Me

Burning like a drop of sun on bare skin
the wave of the past comes with a shock
I had never imagined
or perhaps I didn't want to imagine.

Sometimes, I guess it's not easy to swallow pain
when your mind is flesh
raw as a cut of meat.

Can you say that everything can change for the better
when the air weighs heavily?

This very moment like a noonday moon,
is holding me in its gaze when I try to take myself
out from all of this and start to walk the road
leading toward a distant horizon.

Maybe the mountain will open its door
or maybe the sky will walk in.

Exhibiting bold facts

Then practice losing farther, losing faster:
places, and names, and where it was you meant
to travel. None of these will bring disaster.
            Elizabeth Bishop

We can blame our differences on each other's confusion.
The past already has piled on us volumes of memories,
even to surface from beneath such a depth
is for many a monumental challenge.

How can we reach the unwanted facts
exhibiting the bold reality that they happened anyway
and this reality works in the present time
reproducing itself
            with images like parasites
(giving more reason to detest it)
until they shrink and fall on the ground?

The past sometimes appears as a dreamer,
touching our sensitive nerve to make us
drift between then and now
(its idea of progress).
You can rebel against   bargain anything for a way out
or deconstruct this merry-go-round time machine.

That seems like a calculated assault
but is sky-bellied for the victorious,
for the losers it will be a sobering lesson
proved to be just a tryout.

The Voice of a Bird
in Very Early Morning
for Patty

I was here before   in the night   full
of promises
the best way to know life is
to sip it slowly
like an afternoon tea,
keeping it   with finger tips full of care.
No hurting—no despair.

Your tiny voice
        is touching the end of night
with its longing   and now
I see the light
shifting from one window
                to another
its moon on my pillow
growing.

Being (with) Fiction, Touching Poetry

I am not a tragic romantic
madly in love with grandiose gestures
but attuned to wonder circling around
a virtual mirror of the scene from book
blurring the distinction between
                fiction and the real world.

This is my favourite place:
in the clever manipulation of lines
which redirect
our way of thinking
and break down the boundaries
even when the flow of thoughts stirs the air
silencing for a moment the birds
of paradise.

Flight
for Travis Lane

In my flight
I'm looking for the highest places
to reach the untraveled air
leading to liberty my imperial heart.

I want imagination
to strengthen my wings
and let me enter places
where I can walk on sun-fire—barefoot.

But heaven is too distant
Eden— (I can imagine) too boring
yet I'm not ready for God's interview.

I'm diving into sunrise
to drink from its red cup.

  Air—sky me blue.

Rain in the Room with Mountain
for Jasper

A few drops of rain were tapping the window
and in a minute, they were gone.

There is seldom rain in this town,
and you cannot hear the river anymore.

Now the mountain bathed in sunset
explodes with a firestorm,
breaking the walls and fences into pieces,

the air becomes smoky glass burning,
chained to the window frame.
In spite of this, the evening brought rain.

Water penetrates the air, then soil,
and returns to the clouds
as the life cycle no one can reach.

I'm lying now inside the rain,
my gown green grass
a meadow,
the sky a brook
spiralling water around rocks of time.

This delight of spirit and flesh
impermanent, soon an illusion
(which lives only for a moment), evaporate.

Image-Makers

While others are still caught in sleep,
I'm outside
striking an hour
of the early morning blaze like a bell
to begin the new day,
knowing that dreams demand fruition
where the horizon paints the sky

fresh as metaphor
seeking nothing but self-gratification
(theoretically possible when unrestrained).

In the blurry light of diluted blackness,
few of us when looking for the enlightened flight
will end up lunatics,
missing the point by aiming at the ceiling.

Into the New World

Here I am at the crossroads
with broken cloud lines able to expand
          & feed the sky.
Let's have a dream—each with its life
     ripening inventions
along hedgerows of thought
which carry us like a blank page to be written on
the sound of water I become
to be found only in invented stories
with reference to existence—sometimes a solitary act
of a self-obsessive clown
(his job is to do foolish things to amuse us).
but let theoreticians do the work
and define who we are
behind smiles
when the world around us plays games
using charisma as a sword to clear the way.

Crossing the Border into Manitoba

*One day you finally knew
what you had to do...*
                    Mary Oliver
                    "The Journey"

       i

Wave of wind
hitting the white forehead of a winter day,
the trees disappearing
one by one.

On this journey through a snowstorm
I'm like the blind man
walking with hope humming in my blood.
Say the word

which will move mountains
and open a new valley,
stop the river flow.
Are you listening?

When sky has the face of cold stone,
when fatigue
is leaving tracks of footprints twisting
across the fields racing with a solitary moon.

ii

I've had to leave my village.
Do you know how it feels
to watch your family vanish under rubble
of the house struck by military planes,
when the smoke has an appetite
which devours all breathing air?

Surrounded by night
I'm trying to grab more time now
when fear of the cold
keeps my feet alive
and the knowledge that every moment
under icy sky can easily betray me
with no sound.

Pause in Time

Time yields no shape.
					Emmanuel Kant

Time is clever —cynical perhaps—
enough to satisfy our snobbishness
engaging us in dialogue
with words of wisdom
combining familiarity
& *the other* unseen

allowing us to sing with rain
or walk through a wall of fire.

If These Lines Could Sing
after Krysztof Rapsa

The lines in the painting take us by surprise
in the middle of thought.
And sound of colours full of tension
stimulates our mind
like actors in play.

Turning in different directions
they are inner forces
repeating themselves
taking possession
of their own constructed planes
of painting.

All laws are left behind.

As we are standing outside of space & time
the lines shift us
toward unknown horizons.

I Lack the Inspired Silence

I lack the inspired silence
of the winterscape
when cold evening winds
each gust blows an acrobatic stunt
where poetry
lives in briefly
manifest anxieties
far truer than our own.

But when I enter it
looking for the lines,
to catch dramatic nature,
she treats me
with an irony
by letting me saunter along her path.

Apocalypse

It started as a thought
without affection
as we walked into an old darkness of night
with blazing moon naked like a light bulb
some people call him beggar
—he swears he's not—never asked for money.

How we are born—we die
with breath soft as blossoms that carry us
into the reeds of watery sky, we sink deeper there
to separate soul from our body
left in the world
howling & cursing.
Time goes on and on
turning cities into dust, sun to stone.

let me think of sweet song, see the dancer in me
in the garden I will never outgrow

Why do we need this constant source of awe
championed by new technology to feel alive?
The skin growing over our skin is thickening,
leather-like—you say, that it is a protective skin,
well-weathered to withstand all climate changes
you say, and I will ask you why do you need to wear
this elephant skin resembling stone walls?

touch me fruitful water, run me through
turn me upside down
so I will stand again on my feet

I Was Rescued by Raw Animal Instinct

There was no initiation rite of crying
that thrill of crying, *welcome me world,*
that excitement when we follow
our ancestors marked by their DNA

when I was leaving the depths
of my mother's belly,
my body covered in burning blue
with the force that conjures & sustains life,
feet first like wings into her borderless fear.

A year before, a girl
the forbidden fruit of lovers,
was strangled by
the life line in my aunt's womb,
leaving a shadow of herself in this room
like a harsh light.

But we are all born with animal instinct
which howls out its hunger for life.

Walk through Conversation

After the storm, the swollen soil was sliced by tiny streams.
Every step we took like walking through the fields
of whipped sponges spreading dark bubbles.

But the cliffs facing the sea remained untouched by the water
and were bathing in sunshine
resembling a painting by Monet.

As much as I would like to think that this moment
full of brilliant simplicity
would slow time
and calm this day
this was not to happen.
Life itself took charge
causing a breakdown of the conversation.

At night I was getting ready to run from all this drama,
but found myself going in circles.

Climb and Dream

I tried to climb up my thoughts
but they were slippery
and my feet were made
of stone
but I've learned   oh I've learned
how to chase my own scream.

Disconnecting the Link

Perhaps, I could forget imprinted scenes,
the mercy of the Libyan desert night
at the checkpoint
when with no proper documents
we were questioned
by teenage boys armed with Kalashnikovs
and then let go.

Or the short-lived relief
at the entrance to the camp
to seek refuge
and to find myself in the middle of action
resembling a movie
with bullets crossing the air,
the shout of *Carabinieri*
looking for a man who shot an Albanian.

Or maybe my desperate jump
through a street level window
of the camp building
to save a puppy
hanging from a tree
to learn that life
no longer had songs for him
only blurred eyes with the intoxication
of a luminous sky.

Mission

*"The future is created
by our actions in the present."
Deepak Chopra*

Far away from home
in the patchwork of abandoned streets
your eyes sense nonsense of the situation
casting pain
in the dusted air.
And I ask you to read my lips beloved,

the words that can elevate you
with your feet still on the ground.
Let me take off
your animal skin with its hunger
for fresh blood,
take off from your face
the noble notion painted
by powerful men of Shakespearean character
talking of peace when thinking of war
and playing gods in leisure.

Don't try to identify me.
My name is among your people.
I'm painfully yours.

Flying the Dream

At twelve I believed that I could fly.
That somehow by jumping high enough
and moving my arms quickly I could remain
in air. This happened only in my dreams.

They say we should pull dreams out of sleep
because they hold a key
though will not reveal the secrets within us,
or answer why we must exist
in a life slashed by the razor-sharp events.

In the still darkness a bird sings
from the tree top.
His voice rushing through the air,
open like wings—unstoppable.

Lizard's Song
for Laurence

I can't hear the lizard's song
although it's sitting on his tongue
between him and the garden wall
white flowers
fall
from the tree
and the sun is walking like a god

it must be a fine song in a play
he knows the lyrics well
and have mastered the melody for sure

his song is now stretching up
swinging
            in a trapeze act
like an acrobat
swaying
high above the street
to charm my window   to open it
            and break up the stillness

take me   out   of siesta
and inject me with the thrill
bearing its own weight deep down
inside my body   waiting

In the End of Summer
for Laurence

As hot as it had been lately
summer is slowing.
Edged with the early arrival of evening,
dimmer lights of the sky
hanging between branches.
The smell of ripened fruits
fermenting in long grass
attracting concerts of crickets
looking for a flame
with a hunger for sex.

It all catches us alone, breeds more thoughts,
deeper nights, each one inside another.

Imagine how many times I've come here
sheading my skin, leaving a trace.

Gypsy Love
for Laurence

I am entering gypsy love
    a wild sisterhood
to learn the secret of its art

    oh hear the cries of the wind
on   bent   grasses
    when
I will go inside the fire   oh
   clap your hands & dance   you
the worshiper
              of my desire.

Love Affair (projected as tragic)

Butterflies are white and blue
In this field we wander through
                    Edna Vincent Millay

Her life long love affair
never fades. She is sinking again
in her bed into shades of wonder
constantly evolving like
a Milky Way she is dreaming of meeting
her enchanted prince who will arrive
on a white horse to take her away. As the day
advances unfolding the reality of illusion
she will try to save it,
stopping time by falling asleep.

Back to Freud's Dream

She is revisiting Freud's dream.
Her skills have improved since the last time.

"You don't need to be perfect," she said,
"just follow the rules."

This dream has the body of a bounty hunter
looking for the fugitive,

ready to act in the sweat of the night,
with tongue of bee honey.

She is ready to be found.

Oceans of Drifting Sand
for Laurence

Wind flattens the landscape,
dry riverbeds sending plumes
of golden dust spiralling into the sky
in the grassland
under the camel-torn trees, lions laze waiting
for the night to hunt.
Ancient sea of sand
rolls forever lifting mirages
restless dunes soar with sound and rumble
in symphonic wind
burning plants sending perfume
of delicate roses
at night you are the lion gone hunting
following my steps.

A Dance on the Roof
for Laurence

You will be my clown
in the mask from *Phantom of the Opera*
singing a song from *Cabaret*.
I will be your girl riding on the back of Pegasus
with a pink umbrella.
We will be rich oh rich
with hats full of golden stars
and oh how we will dance
on the roof with the music
of the fiddle in your eyes.

Wild Horses
for Laurence

She is so alive at dusk
on his belly
among the sounds of wild horses running
and suddenly deserted trails of grass
her body in his hands
shimmering
outstretching through each moment

she can now begin a long voyage
running in her veins like sweet wine
leaving the rooms of her sealed mind
and go barefoot in the Madawaska River.

Standing on the shore she takes over the place
for wild horses to run again . . .

Bogoria

This land comes to me again
and I am on my knees
feeling its sandy soil in my hands.
The aroma of wild thyme
evokes the memory of childhood,
of my steps climbing the hills
with racing blood
to feel the jump, the flight,
the turning air
bewitching my body.

Walking Among the Birds

*As each thing says its secret name
it makes a wilderness a mind.*
      Don McKay

The air drums a discordant sound   boom boom
the night fades away   boom boom boom
as we flow into the immortal song of the lake.

We used to sing in the early daylight
if you could only see me walking the pathway
among the birds
in the exuberance of fields
now this pathway grows at my feet
as a road to nowhere

like a whisper for the soul
the dreams still carry us lost travellers
over the crossing from night to day.

Hear the rocks chant, they walk slowly
across the land wrapped in green
their mirrored images rise in water
to mingle with the lake
all elements of nature
for a moment *equal*.

Romancing the Painting

Art does not reproduce the visible—
Klee said—rather, it makes visible.

Only when we open ourselves
to exercise wonder
the painting emerges from the canvas
like a tower of treasure
we have never known,
the architecture of magic
reaching for us with an open hand
or as a field of blooming colours
born through scorched lids of imagination
at the poet's expense.

I cross this land many times,
I float in space,
roll over the touch of sky,
blue drops of rain,
and I walk through the colours
turn them into forms
filled with light.

And I taste a painting.
Like music—a visionary kind
with virtue
luminous and alive
confronted with shapeless air.

Real Life Drawing

Captured in highly realistic drawing
she moved her body
and teased the viewer with a wink.
She was transformed by an artist
from a real-life model
into black-and-white form on paper.
Her manipulation of the man in the room
was hardly more than clowning around,
but revealing her hidden desire
to retrieve what was once taken.
This attempt to recover the past
was meaningless to anyone but her
because her body viewed by so many visitors
in the art gallery
was for them
only another door of artistic vision
open to the public.

Mindfulness of Lake Ontario

With perseverance detailed in the blueprint of water
rising waves of the lake were shifting its forms
mapping what the mind could explore

as if it wants to wake you up beside wise words
with endless possibilities

as if it wants to walk you down
through the gates beyond the patterns of failure
to obtain clarity

it is possible to reach
the thoughts no longer disturbing you
even when your life hooked on painkillers

is still refusing to be drawn into a waiting line
of whitewashed rooms
beating for you an earthquake.

Bee Caught in Amber

*Many hive bees sucking the flowers through holes
bitten in the base of the tube by humble-bees.*
                    Charles Darwin,
                        On the Origin of Species.

I notice a bee lifting her head
caught in the amber of a bracelet.

And I say: *Life* draw a circle around my feet
to keep me in the present.

Morning Talk in Oakville

Morning is unfolding the sky,
becoming a streaming current of light
and falling somewhere between the trees
we pass.

We are quietly walking a slender road,
winding between shrubs and tall grasses,
with thoughts circling for survival
on a thread-like spiral
testing our own vulnerability.

And I say you can judge
the past once again,
the years when the wrong people
entered your door.

You can judge
the days resonating your foolish mistake
when you mistook a shadow
for an enlightened one.

But don't throw yourself
like a stone against the wall.

Drowned in a Hollow Moon

The silence of my dream was unusually impressive.
Its lyrical brilliance had nothing to do
with the virtue of consolation,
rather it acted as an overture to the next scene.

The coming sound transforming
into shape and vision,
sharp high-pitched note
open like a bird's beak
tracking me down hallways of a strange house.

I could hear the steps eaten away by endless dim streets
as I tried to run away from the demons waiting
at the top of an old tree
with no branches but mirrors reflecting my face.

Tenacity of things is known to us. And in dark dreams
it clings to our body, coils around our legs
to make them unable to move an inch.

Abduction always calculates the effect
in order to achieve its goal,
leaving no stones unturned.
They lift me up like a feather drowned in a hollow moon.

The Blueprint of a Lake

Your happiness to be alive
And sorrow that your life is closing.
                    Czeslaw Milosz

It is a place where air stops suddenly
and changes to a silver tone,
then rides toward the horizon, casting shadows
over Lake Ontario,
making us feel
that we're here only half-present
and the rest is left in a dream-like state.

We are now lost in the reflection of clouds,
between the rocks covered by algae over time,
time that is faster than our thoughts
circling the shores of the lake.

I see a school of tiny silver fish at play,
shining like shards of broken glass.
They jump into the air,
then try to hide in the waves.
Effortlessly, the hungry seagulls collect them
bite by bite.

Their performance a reminder
that everything comes to its end
often in the hungry throat of predators
as a vital source of energy
for the need of species to reproduce.
Nature is the force that carries the acts.
She explains her actions,
but will never ask us for forgiveness.

The Tree Dries to Dust

Over the months I watch this tree across the road.
Trapped in new circumstances. Foreigner in its own place.
Persona non grata in the eyes of the developers
cloning houses with one click of a neurotic mouse.

Now the tree stands alone reshaping air. Strong limbs carry the sky
like a feather. The house by its side is erased, betrayed for cash.

Soon lilacs will bloom.

I pledge myself to let unconsciousness take over, go deeper
into the psyche of this tree with furious awareness
that its end will come in the sharp light
of early spring, the grinding chainsaw.

The Buried Side of Childhood

*The psychic life of civilized man, however,
is full of problems.*
                    Carl Jung

1. The Side

Everything is in its place, sculptured like a temple
reflecting my childhood. Consciously, I tried not to touch
its contents ready to speak face to face,
or listen to its stories—until now.

2. The Final Inquest

I'm on my way toward the past
with you, my father I didn't like
to carry out an inquest as part of your redemption.
"Every act performed with justice is a virtue,"
Socrates once said.
My tongue will rise to the words
ready to stand up to you.

3. The King, the Court

You ruled the kingdom of your own insanity.
We were your court
and when requested to show
our acts of devotion
we placed a kiss on your cheek
feeling the despair of Judas.
The peace of our household
was the payment.

4. The End or Consolation

My fingers on eyelids hard-pressed to see the lost time,
where the house could bear songs of children playing
instead the shadows running in the underground rivers
never allowed to see the reflection of the sky.
Now, when you are stripped of the crown
I'm ready to depart
enduring what is left behind.

The Narrow Pathway of Childhood

Angel of hope and calendars, do you know despair?
Anne Sexton,
The Book of Folly

This narrow pathway between two fences
is a chamber containing my childhood.
I can hear my small feet running,
teasing the air darkened by an overgrowth of trees,
laughter opening an exit a few steps from home.

Now, I can only unroll moments
written on a scroll of life.
Do I need to walk again into the room,
and cast off sleepless nights the silence
broken by angry conversation of my parents?
With words clinging to walls
until slowly they diffused.

The home a volcano waiting for the next eruption.
Everything engulfed in menace
flower pots, cans of food,
a broken chair that landed in the wounded air.

I was envious of the ladybug's flight.
Landed on my finger tip, this tiny drop of blood
would miraculously come to life under my spell
with open wings
to free me from walking the earth.

Sitting on an embankment, concealed by tall weeds
I spent days watching trains passing by
if only for a few seconds
I was with them
escaping to undisclosed locations of the countryside
or locking myself in the hidden rooms of far away cities.
With eyes wide open
I searched for the soul of all things
to become one with clouds
raising the music of rain.
How little remains now
of that once so articulate wonder.

Walking the Night

Reluctant to let me in when I try to follow her steps
into the fields caught in a new vision of city planners,
she is out of the shade, covered by ragged rocks
roasted in the sun that offers no luxury.

Walking the night, standing in a galaxy of planets
I search for the original tale of this land
circling around slashed trees,
the streets are closing in,
penetrating our brains to drain them.

The city will sing its rap songs breathing words in and out
the wind veering between buildings
like a shark's fin and the night grows hard as stone.

Each of Us

A low-ceilinged sky
is silently pressing down the snow into the ground
exposing first green shoots. Almond shaped spikes of daffodils
stand propped up against a cold wave of April air.

Our journey began with a first step. It requires more than courage.

We are all grains of sand.
Our common place an uncompassionate hourglass.

My face struck by a sunray feels like a sandy beach,
flaming my brain after a long winter.

Bird, your cardinal coat is ready for you to mate.

Each of us carries nostalgia
yearning in the spring to be of use.
Granted the privilege, they take control over old stuff
buried in the dusty drawers of our minds. Bless imperfections.
The moon will awaken in us the sleepwalkers.

We Are All Immigrants on This Planet
for Darrow Woods

Today the sky is not polite company for my walk.
Moaning, metal grey,
sending down heavy drops of rain,
asking me to run for cover.
Soon the lonesome road
will be turned upside down like a life
with cracks on its surface, a reminder of days
we could not escape.

Disoriented and left in the middle of the road,
having only a single coin in hand,
we toss it straight into the air
with hope of good luck.

I can find you among lost travellers
looking at moments in time, longing to be carried by the clouds
with wings heading home
wherever it is.

We are all one—immigrants on this planet,
the luminescence of wind on dusty roads
with dreams exceeding borders.
All the heroes or potential heroes, kings or queens
ruling from our castles with exhaustion growing.
We are all saints—someone said—and this earth is heaven.

All These Moments of Difficult Truth

Truth appears to satisfy our hunger for knowledge
It clings to events and eloquently explains
what has happened.

It engages us face-to-face with conversation
we were avoiding in the past
by using words still hidden in each other's shadow.

When approaching the harsh nature
of conclusion we reach the emotional
edge facing the ground,

severed like an acidic stone crack,
a blinding eye of the thunderstorm,
in the room with no exit. For the moment.

My acts—they're everybody's
and being bound perpetually to them
we sometimes hear the song of a bird

or the roar of enraged lion
but this depends on our will to listen
which gives us a chance to walk a straight line.

Shreds of Thoughts

Blind and clinging a fog rises. Wind drinks it slowly.
I watch water running under the still frozen skin of stream,
envious of her sense of direction.

We are stuck in the frame of time we can't outgrow.
It is so human to test its limits.

The stage prepared by life's order is equipped with selected gestures.
Words do not always match gesticulation.

Some of us are credited by blind instinct to believe in God's power.
Devotion is a starting point. Prayer a spiritual remedy.

Today I opened the window to a bird's song.

Its soft, enchanted music seduces our brain.
We sing la la la, rocking the universe made of hand-cut
collages of stainless steel.

Birthday cards are claiming a little chunk of our life year after year.
Newborn child is a bird of prey of time.

"Hold me" says the rock, "the cold strips me to the bone."

Moving with the Current

Now we who turn our backs on the past,
feel the years still burning inside of us

though we move with the current of time
which sometimes contradicts our conception of reason.

Your tongue is destined to be harp-like
performing poems in the place
where minds and sounds converge
to find what is meant to be found.

Eva Kolacz Biographical Note:

What circumstances will make a person leave their country, knowing that they will never be allowed to return? What makes a person leave behind everything they possess? What makes a person leave family and friends knowing they may never see them again? In 1981, Eva Kolacz, a young actress and poet, left Poland, then ruled by the Soviet Union, because the voices of artists and writers were silenced by censorship. She couldn't travel freely.

Living behind the Iron Curtain she felt like a bird in a cage. With her daughter she travelled to Libya to join her husband, a civil engineer working under contract. The three of them ran to Italy and spent a few months in the refugee camp, Latina, before immigrating to Canada. Not knowing English, she chose to express herself visually through art and became a professional painter. Her poems were published in Polish magazines. It took her 25 years to write poems in English; this is her first book.

www.ingramcontent.com/pod-product-compliance
Lightning Source LLC
Chambersburg PA
CBHW030130100526
44591CB00009B/590